A Robbie Reader

HARRY STYLES

Mitchell Lane

PUBLISHERS
2001 SW 31st Avenue
Hallandale, FL 33009
www.mitchelllane.com

Tammy
Gagne

Mitchell Lane

PUBLISHERS

Printing   1   2   3   4   5   6   7   8   9

A Robbie Reader Biography

Library of Congress Cataloging-in-Publication Data
Names: Gagne, Tammy, author.
Title: Harry Styles / by Tammy Gagne.
Description: Hallandale, FL : Mitchell Lane Publishers, [2019] | Series: A Robbie reader | Includes bibliographical references and index.
Identifiers: LCCN 2018008725 | ISBN 9781680202885 (library bound)
Subjects: LCSH: Styles, Harry, 1994- —Juvenile literature. | Singers—England—Biography— Juvenile literature.
Classification: LCC ML3930.S89 G34 2018 | DDC 782.42164092 [B] —dc23
LC record available at https://lccn.loc.gov/2018008725

eBook ISBN: 978-1-68020-289-2

ABOUT THE AUTHOR: Tammy Gagne is the author of numerous books for adults and children, including *Shawn Mendes* and *Ed Sheeran* for Mitchell Lane Publishers. She resides in northern New England with her husband and son. One of her favorite pastimes is visiting schools to speak to kids about the writing process.

CONTENTS

Words in **bold** type can be found in the glossary.

In January of 2018, Harry performed as a solo artist at New York City's Radio City Music Hall as part of the MusiCares Person of the Year, which honored Fleetwood Mac.

1

A NEW DIRECTION

Matt and Jesse were prepping for the last middle school dance of the year. As members of the student council, they always helped plan these fun events. They also served as the DJs.

"Can I please have the kitchen table back?" Matt's mom asked. "Dinner is almost ready. You're welcome to stay, Jesse."

Before Jesse could accept her invitation, Matt offered a status report. "Our playlist is almost done. We just need one or two more songs."

"How about the new Harry Styles song?" April suggested as she headed to the table with placemats and silverware.

> **"How about the new Harry Styles song?"**

CHAPTER 1

In the last few years many people have discovered Harry Styles. If they haven't heard his solo music on the radio or music-streaming services, they may have seen him acting in the film *Dunkirk*.

"Now April, it's not nice to tease your brother. You know he doesn't like boy bands." Their mother had heard the kids argue about boy bands in the past. Each time April played her music too loudly, Matt complained. His problem wasn't the volume but rather the artists his younger sister liked. He even joked that he would only play those songs at dances so kids could grab a drink or run to the bathroom without missing the good music. Their mother was rather proud of herself for knowing that Harry Styles had been in a boy band called One Direction. He was April's favorite member of the group.

"Actually," Matt said to his mother's surprise, "Harry Styles is pretty cool. He's on his own now, and his music is great for dancing."

"Excellent," Mom said as she began filling plates. "Harry can stay for dinner, too. We can listen to his new song while we eat."

In the last few years many people have discovered Harry Styles. If they haven't heard his solo music on the radio or music-streaming services, they may have seen him acting in the film *Dunkirk*. The World War II-era movie received many rave reviews from critics. It is unlikely the young singer's last venture into the world of acting. This artistic young man from Great Britain clearly has a wide range of talents to share with his fans, both new and old.

2 WHERE IT ALL BEGAN

Harry Edward Styles was born on February 1, 1994, in Redditch, Worcestershire. The family moved to Holmes Chapel, Cheshire, when he was still a baby. When his mother Anne and father Desmond divorced when he was seven, Harry and his older sister, Gemma, continued to live in Holmes Chapel with their mother. Although Desmond worked in **finance**, he was fond of music. Harry grew up listening to his father's favorite groups such as Pink Floyd and the Rolling Stones. Anne's musical taste was different. She liked Shania Twain and Nora Jones. These different sounds gave Harry a varied taste in music.

> Harry grew up listening to his father's favorite groups.

Proud father Desmond Styles made it all the way to Miami, Florida, to Harry's performance in the One Direction: Where We Are Tour in 2014.

Harry brought his sister Gemma to the Another Man A/W launch. Harry hosted the event, which took place in London, along with Alister Mackie and Kris Van Assche.

It was Anne who encouraged Harry to try out for a televised talent competition called *The X Factor*. While in high school, Harry had been the lead singer of a band called White Eskimo. In 2010, he took a chance by **auditioning** for the British television show. He sang the 1976 Stevie Wonder song "Isn't She Lovely" for the judges, who included Simon Cowell. Cowell had a reputation for being a harsh critic. But he could tell that Harry had a special talent. When he was cut before the finals, Cowell and fellow judge Nicole

Scherzinger had an idea. They handpicked Harry to perform as part of a group with four other competitors as a new group act called One Direction.

Harry and his new bandmates–Niall Horan, Liam Payne, Louis Tomlinson, and Zayn Malik–were now known as One Direction. He was the youngest member of the new group. Audiences instantly embraced One Direction. They had a huge

Harry rose to fame with his One Direction band mates Liam Payne, Louis Tomlinson, Zane Malik, and Niall Horan. They are seen here in 2010 with Simon Cowell during a press conference for The X Factor.

> Some people compared One Direction's overwhelming reception by fans to that of the Beatles back in the 1960s.

following heading into the finals. But they ultimately came in third in the competition. Still, Cowell recognized the band's enormous **potential**. He signed the young men to his recording label after they were eliminated.

After releasing their first album, *Up All Night*, in 2011, One Direction started moving up the record charts in both the United Kingdom and the United States.

Some people compared One Direction's overwhelming reception by fans to that of the Beatles back in the 1960s. In just two years, Harry had gone from a relatively unknown high school student to pop royalty.

3 WATCHING THEIR EVERY MOVE

One Direction's passionate fan base led the group to tremendous success. The group's second album, *Take Me Home*, made it to the top spot on record charts in more than 35 countries. The following year, One Direction's "Where We Are" world tour sold out arenas all over the United States with

more than $230 million in ticket sales. Before the tour's end, those numbers would reach $1 billion. This number beat records previously held by the Rolling Stones and U2.

Of course, being famous can be fun at times.

Of course, being famous can be fun at times. But what fans don't always realize is that being in the spotlight all the time can also feel exhausting and **intrusive**. Not long after One Direction became a household name, the guys started making the news with everything they did. Gossip newspapers were more than willing to print stories about every personal relationship Harry and his bandmates had. When Harry began dating superstar singer Taylor Swift, the media began watching their every move. Eager fans wanted to learn everything they could about the musicians. But most stories missed important details of who the band members were as people.

> Not long after One Direction became a household name, the guys started making the news with everything they did.

For this reason they agreed to shoot a **documentary** about their lives as members of One Direction. As Harry told the British

Having a relationship in the public eye isn't easy, as Harry found out when he dated fellow musician Taylor Swift. The pair is pictured here on a night out together in New York City.

newspaper *The Independent*, "This was really a bit of a thank you to fans really, for sticking with us. We wanted to show them the real us, because social media and interviews don't really give you the chance to get to know someone."

The 3D film, like everything else having to do with the band, was an instant

hit. Called *This Is Us*, it brought fans to movie theaters in droves. Ahead of the film's premiere in London, hundreds of fans even camped in Leicester Square just for a chance to see the band members as they made their way into the theater for the documentary's first showing.

Dunkirk wasn't technically Harry's first movie. The documentary One Direction: This Is Us *was released in 2013. It gave the band's fans a behind-the-scenes look at life as a member of the famous group.*

4 GOING SOLO

After performing together for several years, One Direction decided it was time to take a break in August 2015. The busy schedule that the band demanded had become too intense for all the members. Zayn Malik had already left the group earlier that year. Now the rest of the young men were also ready to move forward and pursue other projects. One Direction's most devoted fans were devastated by this news. Many still hope that the band members might change their minds and reunite at some point in the future.

Harry is open to the idea. He told *Rolling Stone*, "I love the band, and would

One Direction's most devoted fans were devastated by this news.

In August of 2015, Harry performed during ABC's Good Morning America in New York City.

Harry performed his hit single "Sign of the Times" on Saturday Night Live in April of 2017.

> Fans obviously appreciated Harry's first solo effort as much as they enjoyed his work as part of an ensemble.

never rule out anything in the future. The band changed my life, gave me everything." But leaving One Direction gave Harry the opportunity to start a solo career. It also inspired him to change the sound of the music he was making. Instead of recording pop, he wanted to move into rock music.

He also wanted to use his music to share stories that meant something to him personally. Most songs tell stories. But he wanted to tell stories about his own life, his own experiences. The career he was moving toward was one that he felt was more honest. He released his first solo album, *Harry Styles*, in May 2017.

His first single, "Sign of the Times," went straight to number one. In the process it bumped the wildly popular "Shape of You"

Harry traveled to Sydney, Australia, in November of 2017 to accept the ARIA for Best International Act during the 31st Annual ARIA Awards.

by Ed Sheeran out of the top spot after spending 13 weeks there. Fans obviously appreciated Harry's first solo effort as much as they enjoyed his work as part of an **ensemble**. Critics also praised his solo work. Perhaps those One Direction fans wouldn't stay heartbroken for long after all.

5 A SERIOUS ROLE

Making his own music was just the beginning of Harry's new career. He also decided that he wanted to try acting professionally. He had done some acting back when he was in school and deeply enjoyed it. He was also a huge fan of film.

While boy bands often have large followings among young people, artists who begin their careers as part of one are sometimes mocked a bit. It can be difficult for band members to move beyond the boyish image. When Harry received a part in the 2017 movie *Dunkirk*, many people wondered if people would take him seriously as an actor—and if he could in fact act.

> It can be difficult for band members to move beyond the boyish image.

Harry attended the New York premiere of Dunkirk in July of 2017. He played a small role in the World War II drama.

CHAPTER 5

Although his part was a small one, he earned excellent reviews from a variety of sources, from NPR to *Entertainment Weekly*.

One thing Harry's fans are not surprised about is his charitable nature. Ever since his One Direction days, the performer has been involved with some important causes. In 2013, the band recorded a cover version of the Blondie song "One Way or Another" for Comic Relief, a charity that helps fight poverty and homelessness. When Harry was touring in South Africa, he spent time visiting with students at the Lalela Project, which provides art education to disadvantaged kids. He enjoys giving back.

> Harry seems to have mastered the art of singing. And he also appears to be a capable actor.

Harry seems to have mastered the art of singing. And he also appears to be a capable actor. The future is wide open for this talented young man. Whatever his next

Harry lent his talents to the fifth annual "We Can Survive" benefit concert in October of 2017. He performed at the event for CBS Radio in Hollywood, California.

move, he just wants to enjoy his experiences the best he can. As he told *Rolling Stone* in 2017, "I always said, at the very beginning, all I wanted was to be the granddad with the best stories." He has surely racked up his fair share of those already.

CHRONOLOGY

1994   Harry Edward Styles is born on February 1.

2001   Harry's parents get divorced.

2010   Harry enters the televised talent competition *The X Factor*. He joins up with four other contestants on the show to form One Direction. Simon Cowell offers the group a record deal.

2011   One Direction release their first album, *Up All Night*.

2012   The group releases its second album, *Take Me Home*. It tops the record charts in more than 35 countries.

2013   One Direction's "Where We Are" world tour breaks a record with $1 billion in ticket sales. The band releases a documentary called *This Is Us*.

2015   After Zayn Malik's departure, the remaining band members decide to take a break from performing together.

2017   Harry releases his first solo album, *Harry Styles*. He also begins an acting career with a small role in the movie *Dunkirk*.

FIND OUT MORE

Cowen, Elle. *Harry Styles*. Medford, NJ: Plexus, 2013.

Harry Styles. Official website. https://hstyles.co.uk/

One Direction. Official website.
   http://www.onedirectionmusic.com/us/home

WORKS CONSULTED

Allen, Bob. "One Direction Where We Are Tour Breaks $200 Million in Sales." *Billboard*, August 29, 2014. https://www.billboard.com/articles/ business/6236466/one-direction-where-we-are-tour-200-million

Barlow, Eve. "Harry Styles' Solo Album: A Track-by-Track Breakdown." *Variety*, May 12, 2017. http://variety. com/2017/music/news/harry-styles-solo-album-track-breakdown-1202424544/

Chi, Paul. "Why Harry Styles Decided to Launch His Acting Career with Dunkirk." *Vanity Fair*, July 19, 2017. https://www.vanityfair.com/hollywood/2017/07/ harry-styles-dunkirk-premiere

Crowe, Cameron. "Harry Styles' New Direction." *Rolling Stone*, April 18, 2017. https://www.rollingstone.com/ music/features/harry-styles-opens-up-about-famous-flings-honest-new-lp-w476928

"Harry Styles." Biography.com. https://www.biography. com/people/harry-styles-21173991

WORKS CONSULTED

Jones, Emma. "One Direction, one director, one exhausting interview: Harry, Zayn, Niall, Liam and Louis spill the beans on Morgan Spurlock's film This Is Us." *The Independent*, August 20, 2013. http://www. independent.co.uk/arts-entertainment/films/features/ one-direction-one-director-one-exhausting-interview-harry-zayn-niall-liam-and-louis-spill-the-beans-8774860.html

Mandell, Andrea. "Everything critics are saying about Harry Styles in 'Dunkirk.'" *USA Today*, July 20, 2017. https://www.usatoday.com/story/life/ entertainthis/2017/07/20/everything-critics-saying-harry-styles-dunkirk/497778001/

Mills, Sarah. "One Direction launch 3D behind-the-scenes documentary 'This Is Us.'" *Reuters*, August 19, 2013. https://www.reuters.com/article/entertainment-us-onedirection-film/one-direction-launch-3d-behind-the-scenes-documentary-this-is-us-idUSBRE97I0UC20130819

O'Connor, Roisin. "Harry Styles Song 'Sign of the Times' topples Ed Sheeran's 'Shape of You' from No. 1 spot." *The Independent*, April 15, 2017. http://www. independent.co.uk/arts-entertainment/music/news/ harry-styles-sign-of-the-times-number-1-ed-sheeran-shape-of-you-official-charts-album-release-date-a7684811.html

Pocklington, Rebecca. "One Direction set to break record with first $1 billion tour beating U2 and The Rolling Stones." *Mirror*, December 22, 2013. http://www.mirror. co.uk/3am/celebrity-news/one-direction-1-billion-tour-2952857

WORKS CONSULTED

Yam, Kimberly. "Harry Styles Shows That Being Charitable Is Really 'What Makes You Beautiful.'" *Huffington Post*, April 6, 2015. https://www.huffingtonpost.com/2015/04/06/harry-styles-charity-lalela_n_7012802.html

GLOSSARY

audition (aw-DISH-uhn)—a trial given to a performer to decide if he or she is right for a job

documentary (doc-yuh-MEN-tuh-ree)—a film that follows real-life events

ensemble (ahn-SAHM-buhl)—a group of performers who work together

finance (FAHY-nans)—relating to money matters

intrusive (in-TROO-siv)—not invited or welcomed

potential (pih-TEN-shuhl)—possibility to achieve

INDEX

Children's B STYLES
Gagne, Tammy,
Harry Styles /

DEC 2018